CAREER AS AN
EXECUTIVE SECRETARY

ADMINISTRATIVE PROFESSIONAL

EXECUTIVE SECRETARIES ARE THE BACKBONE of any successful organization. You would be hard-pressed to find any productive and accomplished members of a management team who do not have an efficient, well-organized, highly competent executive secretary backing them up.

Often working in the background, but always making their presence felt, executive secretaries, also known nowadays as executive assistants, personal assistants, or administrative professionals, are taking on more responsibility than ever before. Today the job goes way beyond answering phones and taking memos. For instance, with the advent of computers, the duties of the executive secretary have expanded to encompass being an information and communications manager, in addition to the other important tasks these administrative powerhouses handle every day.

In the contemporary management world, executive secretaries often have their own staffs, putting these organizational specialists in the dual role of being in charge of people while also being the confidant and right-hand assistant to high-ranking officials in business, government, and nonprofit organizations. Though executive secretaries do have help, they have to be skilled in every aspect of their job in order to step in and pick up the slack when things get hectic.

This job definitely requires someone who knows something about everything and is willing to learn new things quickly when required. "Can't be done" are not words that are ever uttered by a top-notch executive secretary. You are expected to find ways to make things happen. That is what makes you so valuable in this job. You are the person no one can do without.

Executive secretaries know everything there is to know about the companies, agencies or organizations they work for and they are totally dedicated to the success of these entities. Their input is not only respected but sought out. It is often the executive secretary in an organization who can spot a problem brewing and solve it before it develops into a full-blown crisis. Many executive secretaries are given wide-ranging authority and even hire and fire personnel working for them.

Often overlooked when discussing this job is the sensitive nature of the work done by an executive secretary. People holding this job must be exceptionally trustworthy, as they handle extremely confidential documents, view financial statements seen by only a privileged few, attend private meetings, read personal correspondence, and have access to information that is not in the public domain.

The job title does not come close to describing all the tasks done by an executive secretary. From arranging appointments and scheduling trips to collecting and analyzing important data and preparing reports about it, executive secretaries keep organizations throughout the country running smoothly day to day.

Executive secretaries not only work with the personnel within an organization, they also interact with external contacts, including consultants, vendors, clients, and customers. As executive secretaries prove what they can do, they are often given greater authority and their role within an organization grows, even to the point of being a decision maker on certain matters.

This is not a job you approach without experience. It requires proven clerical, administrative, and management skills. While the responsibilities of an executive secretary may vary from company to company and organization to organization, one thing remains the same – people will be depending on you and you will have to deliver to stay in this fast-paced job.

WHAT YOU CAN DO NOW

IF YOU ARE THINKING ABOUT BECOMING an executive secretary, you have to ask yourself several key questions. Do you have the right temperament? You simply cannot get flustered in this job or lose your patience – ever. Are you detail-oriented? You cannot overlook anything. For some people, it is nerve-racking to make sure every minute detail is checked and rechecked. You simply cannot ever get frazzled or lose focus in this job.

So how do you find out if this job is right for you? Most extracurricular clubs have the position of secretary available, but few people are interested in that job because the office of secretary requires a great deal of work. It is one of the most important positions in a club's hierarchy.

Most people think a club's secretary is only responsible for taking minutes at the meetings, but there is much more to it than that. You maintain all the club's records, except for financial records. You are responsible for sending out, answering, and filing correspondence; setting up meeting dates; sending reminders about meetings; making sure club members are following through on commitments they made to run certain club activities; and numerous other clerical, administrative, and managerial tasks. While the club president charts the course for the club, the secretary is usually the one called on to make sure that agenda is carried out.

Besides volunteering as a club secretary, contact the office of some corporate CEOs in your area or directors of nonprofits. Chances are you will reach their executive secretaries. Ask if any of these executive secretaries will let you shadow them for a few days to see all their job entails on a daily basis at the professional level.

HISTORY OF THE CAREER

INFLUENTIAL PEOPLE HAVE ALWAYS relied on good executive secretaries. During the Middle Ages, for example, high-level secretaries played a major role in wealthy people's lives. These trailblazing executive secretaries handled the private, personal matters of their employers. The job called for a person to be loyal and tight-lipped. Because confidentiality was required, the job was called "secretary," derived from the Latin word "secretum," meaning secret.

Those early executive secretaries were all men, well-educated men, who paid particular attention to detail. They would be considered executive secretaries by today's standards because they addressed just about every issue that arose in their employer's lives, including arranging meetings and taking notes about important business transactions. Knowing some kind of shorthand was a worthwhile skill even in those days. These secretaries became trusted advisors to their employers, many of whom were in government – some heads of state.

In the United States, men maintained their dominance over secretarial jobs from colonial days until the American Civil War (1861-1865). With so many men going to the battlefield and dying during the War Between the States, however, it was difficult to fill clerical jobs throughout the nation. The manpower shortage was causing a workforce crisis nationwide, so in April 1862 US Treasury Secretary Francis E. Spinner took a bold step. He hired a woman, Jennie Douglas, to bolster the workforce at the Treasury Department. On her first day on the job, she accomplished so much that Spinner decided to hire more women, and by the end of the year 70 women were on staff. He paid the women well and kept them on the job even after the war. More government agencies and private businesses began employing women, especially for clerical jobs.

By the late 1800s and the early 1900s, there were more women in secretarial jobs than men. One invention that propelled women into the secretarial field was the first commercially produced typewriter, manufactured by E. Remington & Sons in 1874. While the typewriter could be used by anyone, Remington hired young women to demonstrate the product to potential customers and people began to associate the machine with female workers.

At the turn of the 20th century, some argued that women's nimble fingers made them better typists than men. The author of the Practical Course in Touch Typing (1904), Charles E. Smith, said that the "extremely large and strong fingers," on men's hands made it hard for male typists to use a keyboard, giving women a decided advantage when using the machine. Studies would later prove that both men and women are equally adept at using a typewriter, but the connection between woman and machine had been forever established.

As business continued to boom in the early 20th century, the executive secretary became a crucial member of the management team. Business leaders needed a good executive secretary to handle all the paperwork and keep the day-to-day operations of a company's office working efficiently. When the United States entered World War I in 1917, women entered the workforce in increasing numbers, many filling the remaining clerical jobs held by men who were once again off to war.

By the 1930s, women dominated the office workforce, many as executive secretaries. They did more than just type and take shorthand. Executive secretaries performed the role of office managers.

In 1942, the National Secretaries Association (NSA) was formed in Kansas City, Missouri. The organization gave secretaries a national voice and professional standing. It also established the first certification test for secretaries in 1951, setting a standard of excellence for the profession. The NSA changed its name in 1998 and is now known as the International Association of Administrative Professionals.

In the 1950s, there just were not enough executive secretaries to meet the demand. The US workforce had declined due to a drop in the birth rate during the Depression era (the 1930s). Many jobs went unfilled, and business leaders were begging for help. The good news was the executive secretaries who were on the job during that period could demand top dollar and exceptional fringe benefits.

With the baby-boom generation following the end of World War II, in 1945, the ranks of the workforce swelled and, by the 1970s, jobs for executive secretaries were harder to come by. The competitiveness of the job market meant that those looking to become executive secretaries in the late 20th century were getting better training. Most attended secretarial schools, but many went on to college to study business and take computer science courses.

The additional schooling enhanced their job prospects, as all types of technical equipment started coming into the workplace. Employers were looking for well-trained people to take their companies into the information age, with creative ideas for incorporating the latest technology in their organizations.

Technological advances added new tasks for executive secretaries. Research became part of the job, as well as interpreting all the information-inundating executives, and incorporating it into daily operations. Communications became an even bigger part of an executive secretary's job.

Men are reentering the field and job titles are changing to reflect that. The future seems bright for the tech-savvy professional executive secretary or executive assistant, now needed by those in upper management more than ever before.

WHERE YOU WILL WORK

AS AN EXECUTIVE SECRETARY, YOU CAN CHOOSE a workplace from among a wide range of companies, government agencies, and nonprofit organizations. You are free to work in whatever field interests you the most.

For example, you want to work in government and have a passion for consumer affairs. In most states, residents can turn to a state office of consumer affairs, in addition to local offices in many counties and large cities. The directors of these agencies usually have executive secretaries working for them.

In the corporate sector, you might be fascinated by work in the pharmaceutical industry. The CEOs, vice presidents, and other members of the management team in pharmaceutical companies all have executive secretaries on staff. The same is true of most major companies in every industry, and many small ones as well.

In the nonprofit sector, you can immerse yourself in a cause and be part of an organization working to make the world a better place. As an executive secretary in this sector, you will be rubbing elbows with professionals dedicated to helping other people and advocating for social justice, as well as drawing on the energy of volunteers who come forward to support the effort.

Just think of all the places where executive secretaries work – banks, colleges, hospitals, insurance companies, publishing houses, religious institutions, media outlets, law firms, retail store headquarters, real estate offices, law enforcement, government agencies at all levels, nonprofits of every ilk. The list goes on and on. So you will be able to find a job without having to relocate. If you do want to move to another region, there will be openings for executive secretaries in those locations as well.

From big cities to small towns, organizations of every size and type employ executive secretaries. If the hubbub of a big city calls to you, opportunities for employment abound in busy urban areas. If a more serene setting, in a picturesque suburban or rural town, suits you better, keep in mind that executive secretaries work in those locations, too.

In your search for a job as an executive secretary, do not exclude any locales. Many large corporations have their offices in rural areas where you might not expect to find them.

While executive secretaries work in offices, that workplace setting varies from job to job. If you land a job with a professional sports team, your office would be in a stadium or an arena. A manufacturing plant would be the job site if you worked for a manufacturing firm. A studio would be the backdrop for executive secretaries who are employed by a television or radio station. You can end up on a campus, in a skyscraper, in a business park, or in a storefront.

Do not be fooled into thinking that you will spend all of your time behind a desk. Depending on what type of organization you work for, you will probably be on the move quite often, connecting with other staff members, and making sure the policies and programs put in place by your boss and other members of the organization's management team are being implemented and are working well.

THE WORK YOU WILL DO

THE WORK OF AN EXECUTIVE SECRETARY, once easily defined, is now constantly evolving, in large part because of changing technology. Yet despite all the technological advancements seen over the last few decades, high-level business leaders still do not like typing their own letters or spending time answering endless emails or filing documents.

So typing and filing, as well as taking some dictation, are still in the mix when it comes to the job description for an executive secretary. However, executive secretaries now have a variety of added responsibilities, including recommending – and eventually placing the order for – the latest technology for the modern office. That includes computers, printers and other peripherals, and telephone and videoconferencing systems.

One of the most common purchases executive secretaries recommend is the latest office software. Making decisions on what office software to purchase is no easy task. Executive secretaries must be thoroughly familiar with the capabilities of the software the company or organization currently uses – and any flaws inherent in it. Then they have to evaluate whether proposed new software will address those problems, create any new problems, and have an overall positive impact on the office and the way it is run.

If you bring in new office software, you are expected to teach everyone in the office how to use it. The executive secretary is generally the first person other employees call to help resolve software glitches and to ask for help in repairing broken equipment.

Another new facet of the work done by executive secretaries was introduced by the Internet. Many executive secretaries are called on to do extensive online research and write reports about their findings. This research may involve anything from investigating new products coming to market to checking out news about competitors or reviewing comments being made by the public about the company or organization on social media. Sometimes the executive secretary uses this research to produce presentations for company meetings, annual reports, or community outreach efforts. So writing reports and making clear presentations have become part of today's executive secretary's responsibilities.

For the most part, written follow-up to letters or emails are handled by executive secretaries. So you will be doing constant writing. However, if the person you work for writes his/her own responses to emails or snail mail, or even writes speeches or reports, part of your job will be editing that written work.

Overseeing and managing websites are often part of the work done by contemporary executive secretaries. Executive secretaries may not write the content and usually do not update the websites themselves, but they keep track of this work to see that it gets done in a timely fashion. Working with web designers and content providers, they decide what to include on the website and how it should look. Making sure a website is visually appealing and easy to navigate is also part of the job.

Information management now comes under the purview of executive secretaries. This includes storage and retrieval of data, as well as maintaining and updating entire databases. In addition, in your role as liaison between the chief executive officer and members of the board of directors, other members of the management team and lower-level employees, and outside vendors, it is your job to provide these individuals with any information they request in order for them to properly go about their jobs and fulfill their duties.

For some, answering the telephone may not seem like an important task, but when you are answering the phone for the president of a company or the director of a nonprofit organization, you are setting the tone for the entire enterprise. In essence, you are the voice of the organization. People who call upper management expect to reach someone who is knowledgeable, concerned, efficient, and ready to respond to their needs. Executive secretaries have to convey all that and more.

In screening calls, you make decisions about which calls you can handle by yourself, which calls you direct to specific senior managers, which calls you have to consult with your boss about, and which calls your boss has to handle personally. You are the voice of reason and authority. In this job you have to understand every caller's concerns and problems, and then try to come up with an answer or find a resolution. These calls may be coming from anyone, from department heads to clients to members of the news media. When callbacks are promised, you must see that they are made.

Follow-up is a vital part of the job. Whether that follow-up is by phone, by letter, by email, or via social media, it has to be done and that is your responsibility. The CEO might forget to do something, but you cannot. You are the safety net, making sure that nothing is overlooked.

That is where organization comes in. Well-organized executive secretaries keep minute-to-minute ledgers or, more simply, to-do lists, checking tasks off as they are completed and adding assignments as the need arises. Nothing slips through the cracks.

As an executive secretary, you might have a staff of your own. In that case, you hire, train, direct, and oversee that staff, giving out assignments and seeing that the work is completed on time and up to your standards.

Executive secretaries are in charge of maintaining an accurate inventory of office supplies and ordering supplies when needed. This keeps the office running smoothly and projects moving forward on schedule. When you do not have the necessary supplies on hand, you might not be able to complete a job on time. For example, running out of ink cartridges for the printer can stop work in its tracks. Monitoring expenditures and keeping office records are other aspects of the work done by the executive administrative assistant.

Executive secretaries coordinate the schedule for a CEO, corporate president, director of a nonprofit, or other members of senior management. Appointments and meetings take planning. They have to be scheduled according to priority, and many of these get-togethers involve a number of people. Synchronizing everyone's schedule is complicated, but canceled meetings or holding meetings that an important person cannot attend wastes everyone's time. Ensuring that these meetings come off without a hitch is crucial, and executive secretaries are the people who make that happen.

They are charged with the responsibility of making sure these meetings are productive by drawing up agendas, based on information given to them by the person calling the meeting. Whether this is for a meeting of senior executives, the corporate board, or all the employees, executive secretaries see to it that meeting participants have all the necessary supporting materials they need before the gathering.

Executive secretaries are present at these meetings, taking notes and keeping minutes. After the meeting concludes, they type up and send these minutes to all the participants as soon as possible. If, during the meeting, certain participants are given assignments or volunteer to take on particular tasks, the executive administrative assistant follows up with these individuals and keeps tabs on the progress being made on these undertakings. Then, before another meeting is held, management is made aware of what has been accomplished between meetings and is prepared to address any issues that might have come up in the interim.

Everything that goes on at these meetings is done with an eye towards time management. Meetings start on time, stay on point, and end when they are supposed to. One meeting is usually followed by another because if one meeting is delayed it throws the schedule off for the entire day. So you focus your efforts on keeping everything moving on schedule.

Your creativity will come into play when planning special events, whether it is the launch of a new product line, a corporate party following a big success, or an event to help a worthy cause in the community. The executive secretary is usually the go-to person when it comes to putting these events together. Once again, the company is relying on your organizational skills to ensure that these events come off flawlessly, bolster pride in the company, and boost employee morale.

Depending on their experience, many executive secretaries today are responsible for running the day-to-day operations of a company or organization. It is imperative for you to thoroughly understand the inner workings of the company or organization where you work, and the field your organization is engaged in. The decisions you make have to be in line with company policy and the philosophy of the CEO, president, or director. You can never lose sight of your main goal, which is to provide administrative support for the person you are working for and help make that individual more productive.

Legal and medical executive secretaries are a separate category. Though they have many of the same duties as their counterparts in other fields, some major differences set them apart. Legal and medical executive secretaries go through specialized training. Rarely is the terminology in other businesses as complicated as it is in either the legal or the medical world. An executive administrative assistant has to have legal or medical terms down cold in order to succeed in these fields.

Legal Secretary

Executive secretaries in law offices, for example, work on many legal documents, including motions, complaints, affidavits, deeds, subpoenas, contracts, briefs, plea bargains, appeals, divorce papers, wills, child custody agreements, and many more. They help prepare these papers, proofread them, make sure nothing is omitted, arrange to have the parties sign them, file them, and make sure all sides involved get copies of the papers. If documents for a case need to be tracked down, you have to try to find them.

In addition, executive legal secretaries are usually present at meetings with clients, taking copious notes of everything that is said, so the attorney can review the notes after the meeting in order to further advise the client. If, after reviewing the notes, the attorney has some follow-up questions for the client, the executive secretary usually contacts the client to fill in the holes.

Keeping accurate records of evidence in a case is another task that falls to the executive legal secretary, as is reviewing law journals for precedent-setting information that might pertain to the branch of law practiced at the firm.

Maintaining a lawyer's files that are taken to and from court each day during a trial is vital, as is adding any new information and typing up each day's notes. Many executive legal secretaries attend trials and are often given assignments based on how the court action proceeds on any given day.

Retaining records in connection with the billable hours for each case, and all expenses involved with that case, is also the job of the executive secretary in a legal office, along with maintaining an up-to-date accounting of all escrow accounts. One of the most important aspects of the job is updating the office calendar and making sure attorneys are aware of court appearances and return dates for court filings and pleadings.

Medical Secretary

Medical executive secretaries can work in a small or a very large doctor's office. You could work for one or several doctors. You could also work in a hospital, a clinic, or a medical research foundation.

Some of the aspects of the job include making sure a patient's medical records contain all the latest information. That includes tracking down the results of tests that have been recently taken. If several tests are taken, it is the job of the executive administrative assistant to prepare an overall report on all the tests, so the doctor can review them quickly. In this post, you will consult with other doctors' offices to include those physicians' notes in the patient's file.

Many doctors record their findings and recommendations for each patient on a small recorder, and you will have to transcribe those notes quickly and accurately, especially if they are needed by another doctor or hospital. If appointments need to be coordinated with several specialists, you have to get the scheduling done.

Oftentimes, the executive secretary meets with representatives from pharmaceutical companies to discuss the pluses and minuses of certain drugs patients have been using. Your job also includes arranging meetings with other physicians when needed and working with the doctor on any speeches and lectures the physician is asked to give at medical conferences.

EXECUTIVE SECRETARIES TELL ABOUT THEIR WORK

I Am the Executive Secretary for the Chief Executive Officer of a Hospital

"I think every executive secretary's job is a bit different. You must have the standard clerical and managerial skills to get the work done, but then there are those special responsibilities and assignments you are given, many often based on specific talents you bring to the job.

I am surprised by how much writing I do in my job as an executive secretary. I always liked to write and even had some articles published before I ever got this job. I never thought it would be an integral part of my job as an executive secretary.

I noted my writing skills on my résumé and that caught the attention of the person at the hospital looking to hire an executive secretary. Some executives like to write their own letters and reports and some don't. The person I work for was thrilled that I had a background in writing and, for this job at least, that gave me an edge in getting hired.

Sometimes the person I work for likes to write his own letters and he asks me to edit them for him. The editing involves checking the basics, like spelling, punctuation, grammar, and run-on sentences. I'm another set of eyes.

For the most part, however, my boss leaves the writing up to me. He gives me a list of salient points and asks me to put a correspondence together for him. My boss then reviews and signs off on the letter.

He also asks me to do research on a variety of topics and write reports about what I've found out. Those reports usually end up in the hands of the board of directors or department heads. So the reports have to be well researched as well as well written.

I urge executive secretaries to take the time to really get to know the field they are working in. I was not particularly familiar with the medical field and all the terms used in the profession. So I studied the field a bit when I first started this job, and got some help with terminology from nurses I became friendly with at the hospital. When you speak to me now, you'd think I had gone for some medical training but, of course, I didn't.

It took some work, but it was all well worth the time and effort I put in to learn about the medical field, get a grasp of the terminology, and understand hospitals as a business entity. That knowledge helps me write better reports and letters. It allows me to fit in and communicate better with the people who work here. In addition, I can sound authoritative, which is important in this job. I'm treated as an equal by doctors and other medical staff, as well as by administrative executives at the hospital.

I speak with many executive secretaries these days who have the added task of doing research for their bosses. While the ability to do research is not something that readily comes to mind when thinking about the skills needed to be an executive secretary, being a good researcher is a talent that is highly respected by those hiring executive secretaries today."

I Am the Executive Secretary for the Director of a National Nonprofit Organization

"This is a job for somebody who likes to keep busy. There's a great deal to get done between administrative, clerical, and managerial work, and it's up to me to get it all done.

Very often, the executive director and the assistant executive director are both out of the office at the same time, giving speeches about the organization to various groups or meeting with corporate sponsors or private donors who want to make large contributions. On those occasions, I am running the office, so there is a lot of responsibility that comes with this job. These people put their trust in me and I don't want to let them down.

I have support staff and I hire those individuals. I have to be able to identify talent and choose good people who can back me up during our most hectic times. The people who work for me have to be versatile and flexible. There is very little downtime.

I think time management is very important. When you get some experience on this job, you learn how vital it is to your daily success to know where everything is in the office. You don't want to hunt around for a year-end report all day.

Equally as important is knowing who to assign to a task to get it completed properly and without delay. That includes outside vendors as well. If I need to make travel arrangements for a member of our management team, I have to know that the travel agent I work with can make those arrangements quickly and, if need be, change them just as quickly. I have a team of both in-house people and outside vendors who are my go-to people. I do the impossible because they can do the impossible.

There is much more decision-making in this job than I ever thought possible. I am really the link between the public, most of the staff, and our management team. I hear about most of the problems first. If someone calls up with an issue, I try to resolve it either myself or by getting a member of the organization's staff involved who can handle it. I follow up to make sure the issue gets resolved. Problems really only go to the executive director or assistant executive director if it's a major policy decision or a matter we just can't get settled without involving top management. The decisions I make have to be in line with the policies and thinking of the organization and the executive director.

I've found that, with many of these issues, it comes down to how fast we respond and letting people see we are taking action or at least trying to take action. Lots of times these matters require a personal touch, and I try to provide that. We are here to help people and I think people want to see that we care, we take an interest in a problem, and we are dedicated to finding a solution.

With all that said, I am still the one who goes around and makes sure we have all the supplies we need and that all the routine matters – like replying to both emails and written correspondence that we get in the mail – are handled and copies are filed properly. I don't do all that myself, but the buck stops here, so it's my job to make sure that it all gets done.

I don't think many people, who have never done this job, realize how critical it is to any organization – public or private – that this job is done efficiently. To me, it's the ultimate behind-the-scenes work."

I Am the Executive Secretary for the President of a Corporation

"You have to come to this job with an inborn trait – organization. I have always been a very organized person. I don't think you can be taught that. I believe great organizational skills come naturally to a person and putting things in order can't be viewed as drudgery. You have to be able to look at things in disorder, see a way you can bring some kind of organization to it all, and enjoy doing that. You view it as an accomplishment.

When I first started this job 14 years ago, everything was here, but there was just general disarray. It made the job that much harder. We'd spend hours searching for important reports, correspondence, and other documents. That was wasted time, resulting in other things not getting done as the search went on.

I established a filing system that works. I believe if something is worth keeping, then you should know where it is. That meant tearing everything apart and putting it back together again. I think everyone here thought I was crazy until they started using my system and saw how well it works.

Not every executive secretary starts a job and has to build or rebuild a filing system or completely reorganize an office. Sometimes an executive secretary retires and hands you an office that runs like a fine-tuned machine, but you have to maintain that system or any system. That means you don't leave jobs like filing for later. You do it right away and get it done before clutter begins to build and things start to get misplaced. When you are organized, things just get done faster and the whole office is more efficient.

You set the example. If you let something slide, or don't put it back right away, others quickly follow suit. It is very easy to get disorganized and hard to regain that structure to keep everything orderly. When I go on vacation, I make sure the person who fills in for me is as organized as I am, or I return to mayhem.

There is a knack to having an organized office. You have to establish a system that everybody, including your boss, is comfortable with. It has to be simple to follow and work for everyone. Complicated just frustrates everybody and people don't want to bother with it. Everybody has to see how well the system works and how it makes life in the office easier.

Executive secretaries run the office. If something isn't going well, I'm usually the one who spots it first. I either make changes or, if the issue is serious enough, bring the problem to the attention of my boss.

Executive secretaries are very hands-on. They know the day-to-day operation of a company inside and out. If there are policy changes made by the president, it's the executive secretary who usually lets everyone know about it. So you walk a very fine line. You have to be authoritative but also approachable. "

"You are really an extension of the executive you work for. Your persona on the job has to be a blend of the personality of that person and your own. In other words, if the boss is more casual, the atmosphere is more relaxed; if the person is rather rigid, the mood in the workplace is more formal."

PERSONAL QUALIFICATIONS

TO BE AN EXECUTIVE SECRETARY YOU have to be an outstanding multitasker. You will be juggling many responsibilities at the same time. Establishing priorities and making quick adjustments as situations change are key to succeeding in this job. Multitasking is probably the second-most important skill you need as an executive secretary, right after being extremely well organized.

Honesty and integrity are high on the list as well. You will have access to a wide array of confidential information and you will be expected never to discuss or divulge this information to anyone, except your boss – not even your closest family members.

Superior time management skills will not only help you get things done, but they will keep the schedule of the person you work for running smoothly. You are the one responsible for making sure meetings start and end promptly, and that materials are prepared for those meetings, so no time is wasted.

A friendly and pleasant personality is a must. Executive secretaries can never lose their composure, must always be tactful and respectful, and have to show plenty of patience. At the same time, in this job, you have to know when to be authoritative and direct.

This is a position for clever problem solvers. Every day, some type of crisis arises. There is no time to get flustered. Solutions are required and, more often than not, you are the one who will have to come up with them.

With technology often changing faster than people can keep up with it, you will always be learning something new. Executive secretaries must be quick studies. You have to be open to updating your skills all the time. For example, you will have to master every new method of communication as it is introduced. In addition, you have to know how your company or organization can benefit by using that means of contact.

Today, executive secretaries are in charge of making sure every piece of office equipment is up and running and able to perform the latest task. If something breaks, you either must know how to fix it or who to call to get it fixed – ASAP.

As an executive secretary, you have your finger on the pulse of the latest issues that affect your company and the field your company is in. Monitoring changing developments in the field, as well as staying on top of how the latest economic and social trends impact the organization you work for, helps make you indispensable.

Successful business leaders rely heavily on the insights and advice offered by executive secretaries. That is because these high-ranking administrative aides are on the front lines. They spend a great deal of their time working directly with staff, customers, and visitors to the company. In this job, you find out firsthand what people are thinking and what they would like to see done. So, add being a good listener to the list of necessary qualifications for this position.

Good communications skills are vital for any executive secretary – writing, in particular. Responding to emails and posts on social media, updating websites and social network pages, even writing blogs for their bosses – these skills are often required of an executive secretary.

ATTRACTIVE FEATURES

IF YOU LIKE BEING BUSY AND LOOKING BACK at all you accomplished by the end of the day, a job as an executive secretary will not disappoint. No two days are ever alike, so you never get into a rut. You rarely have a dull moment, and you are always on the move.

This job presents new challenges every day. It gives you the opportunity to find creative ways to solve problems while making the office run more efficiently.

You will leave your mark on the organization you are working for and have a real impact in your job. Major business publications have called executive secretaries the "most powerful people in the office" and "the CEO's secret weapon." You make it possible for the people in charge to do a better job and be at the top of their game.

No matter what else is going on in the office, executive secretaries are making things happen and getting work done. There is no gridlock on your watch. It is your job to keep everyone focused and that makes you integral to the organization.

Freedom abounds in this job. You do your tasks or assign them to other people who work for you in any order you see fit. You have the autonomy to prioritize things and take care of them in order of importance.

Executive secretaries who do their jobs well do not have to worry about job security. No boss is going to replace the person who makes him/her look good to everyone in the office and everyone in the field.

The skills you use as an executive secretary, as well as many of the pointers you pick up while on the job, are highly transferable to other jobs. You would be a valuable addition to any organization in a variety of posts.

You may not get a thank-you all the time, but when you do, it will really mean something. Those kinds of kudos usually come after you have done the impossible. You can take pride in everything your company, agency, or organization accomplishes because you have a hand in it all.

You are always helping people. Whether it is coworkers, outside vendors, or customers and clients, you are providing a service and finding solutions to intractable problems. You keep the whole operation on track.

You have your pulse on everything that is going on in your workplace. News about who is leaving, who is getting promoted, and the bottom line on how the organization is doing usually crosses your desk first.

One of the perks in this job is that you make innumerable contacts. Meeting all the movers and shakers in your industry is par for the course. You generally attend conferences with all the key leaders in the field, sometimes even well-known political leaders and celebrities. Upon meeting these people and telling them what you do, they will know you are both talented and trustworthy. More than anyone else, these people realize how important executive secretaries are to the success of the entire enterprise and respect the work you do.

UNATTRACTIVE ASPECTS

BEING AN EXECUTIVE SECRETARY CAN be a very stressful job. If your boss has a problem, you are expected to solve it. These dilemmas can crop up out of nowhere and catch you by surprise. You always have to respond quickly. Sometimes it's a problem you and your boss have to solve together. Other times it all falls back on you.

Pressure may be intense in this job on particular days, especially if you work for or with people who come unraveled when things go wrong. Technology can often work against you, as you get inundated with emails every day, and everybody expects an immediate answer. That just adds to the pressure you feel in this job, and just imagine what happens when the computer system goes down.

You are going to come across people who have difficult personalities. They might not understand all the work you have to do, and become annoyed that you did not get their project done fast enough. Some people expect you to drop everything and turn your attention to their project or problem immediately, and often that is not possible.

As an executive secretary, you do so much behind the scenes to keep a company or organization running efficiently that many executives and other employees just do not realize all you do. Being underappreciated is a feeling many executive secretaries wrestle with. Most people on the job do not thank you when everything is going well, but are quick to blame you if something goes awry, even if it is not your fault.

In this job you have to be happy working in the background, knowing you had a big hand in the success of a project or the overall success of the organization, and be satisfied with that. People are going to take credit for the work you did. Even if you did most of the work on a project, if your boss spearheaded the undertaking, that is who will get the majority of the credit for the work, even if you are publicly thanked for your "assistance" with it. Being in the shadows is part of the job.

You will have busy seasons and days when the wheels come off everything. If your boss stays late to address these problems, you are probably going to be asked to stay late as well. The overtime hours can come at the most inconvenient moments in your life, but since your boss relies on you, you are going to play an integral part in quelling the crisis. So, like it or not, overtime is part of this normally nine-to-five job.

Executive secretaries are on the front lines. When irate people call your boss, they are most likely going to speak to you first, and you will probably be the target of angry rants. Whether these callers are customers, vendors, or other employees, they are going to want to vent to someone. This could be the toughest part of the job, as you try to get to the root of the problem, calm the person down, and resolve the dispute before your boss or anyone else on the management team has to get involved.

EDUCATION AND TRAINING

THE MINIMUM EDUCATIONAL REQUIREMENT to be a secretary is a high school diploma. Today, if you want to be successful, you will be focused on moving up the corporate ladder quickly. So you still also need to get on-the-job training and experience. If you are lucky, your high school will offer some kind of secretarial skills courses, and you will want to pay attention in English and math class, too. Those lessons will certainly come in handy.

The job market for secretaries is competitive these days. Those in charge of hiring entry-level secretaries with an eye toward having them advance rapidly through the ranks to become executive secretaries or executive administrative assistants are looking for people with some additional education beyond high school. Secretaries may come into the field with a bachelor's degree, most often in a major that is related to the industry they are hoping to work in. That certainly helps them advance to an executive administrative assistant job faster, and perhaps even allows them to go beyond that job title.

However, the most common educational goal in the field is either a certificate or an Associate of Allied Science (AAS) degree in administrative assistant and secretarial science, office administration, or office technology. These courses of study are affordable and geared mostly to the field you are planning to enter. Certificates or associate degree programs are offered at many vocational and technical schools, as well as a number of community colleges throughout the nation. Certificate programs take about a year to complete, and AAS degrees typically require two years.

Both a certificate program and an AAS degree address the latest skills needed to be successful in the secretarial field and get promotions to the higher levels of administrative work. Keep in mind that the AAS is a more in-depth program. Besides mastering the basics needed to run an office, these programs generally offer courses in Business Accounting, Corporate Communication, Office

Management, Record Keeping, Filing-System Development, Report Preparation, Maintaining Spreadsheets, and Presentation Skills. They also provide extensive computer training with a wide range of software applications, from desktop publishing to database management. In addition, some schools have courses in maximizing the use of other office equipment, including telephone and videoconferencing systems.

When you are deciding on which school to attend, make sure the educational institution you are considering has a good-sized computer laboratory. Look into whether the laboratory has the latest equipment and software, and make sure you can schedule plenty of time to work on the computers and get real-time training in both using the computers and learning how to fix simple problems.

Internships are another important aspect of any associate degree program, and many schools with administrative assistant and secretarial school programs now offer these internships so students can gain real-world experience. A good example of this course of study is the two-year Office Administration Program at Alamance Community College in Graham, North Carolina. Courses include Records Management, Text Entry and Formatting, Administrative Office Transcription, Keyboard Skill Building, and Administrative Office Management. Emphasis is put on both nontechnical and technical office skills.

Kansas City Kansas Community College (KCKCC) has a robust program for people looking for training as administrative office professionals. There is a one-year certificate curriculum giving you 32 credits in subjects covering a variety of office-related topics, including Customer Service, Business Communications, and Microcomputer Business Software. KCKCC also has a more extensive two-year program, which results in an associate degree in office administration. That program requires earning 62 credits. Both these programs are offered on campus and online.

A list of schools with similar programs can be found on the college partners' page of the International Association of Administrative Professionals (IAAP) website. A number of schools offer online classes in office administration and many allow students to work at their own pace, though there are deadlines by which coursework must be completed and exams are given.

Vocational and technical schools also offer special training for people who want to become executive secretaries or administrative assistants in the legal or medical field.

Equally as important as education for those looking to become executive secretaries or executive administrative assistants is getting the proper certification. Administrative professionals who pass an exam given by IAAP earn the title of certified administrative professional (CAP). This certification must be renewed every five years.

There are certifications for both medical and legal secretaries as well. The National Healthcare Association certifies medical administrative assistants. So does the American Association of Medical Assistants. Certification is available for legal secretaries from NALS, the association for legal professionals, as well as the Association of Legal Administrators and Legal Secretaries International.

EARNINGS

THE SIZE AND SUCCESS OF THE COMPANY or organization where you work generally dictate your salary as an executive secretary. Experience is part of the equation as well. A highly experienced executive secretary can start out at $55,000 a year, while a person with less experience may be offered $45,000 a year for the same position.

It is not unusual for an executive secretary at a major corporation, who has been with the company a long time, to bring home an annual wage of between $70,000 and $75,000. Recently, it was reported by USA Today that executive secretaries in Silicon Valley start out at $60,000 a year and could earn as much as $150,000 a year, depending on the responsibilities associated with the job.

In addition, executive secretaries at corporations earn bonuses that can range from $500 to $5,000 a year, and often participate in profit- sharing. As an executive secretary, you are privy to how the company is doing, so you will always know what the profits and losses are on an annual basis.

Executive secretaries usually receive a substantial benefits package, including health insurance. At major corporations, they may also receive pension benefits.

The bottom line comes down to how valuable you are to the organization. Keep in mind that CEOs who make millions of dollars a year often have executive secretaries who have worked with them for years. These longtime executive secretaries usually earn in the $100,000 a year range.

In the government and nonprofit sectors, executive secretaries tend to earn somewhat less than those working in the corporate world.

OPPORTUNITIES

OUTSTANDING EXECUTIVE SECRETARIES are always in high demand. Throughout the country, more than 2.3 million executive secretaries are employed full time, including those specializing in the medical and legal fields.

The opportunities for executive secretaries are constantly growing, as new industries, like the tech sector, expand their operations. As these businesses develop, CEOs rely more and more on the skills of executive secretaries to help build the company and boost overall productivity. The US Department of Labor projects a nine percent yearly growth in executive secretary jobs over the next decade.

Executive secretaries complement the efforts of CEOs, doing important jobs these high-level executives just do not have time to handle. Those jobs include answering emails and other correspondence in a timely fashion so the executive does not miss any promising opportunities coming the company's way. With so many contemporary methods of communication, people expect fast replies to their inquiries, and that makes the role of an executive secretary especially crucial.

The information age has made the position of executive secretary even more vital than ever before. Companies need to collect all the information that impacts on the organization and the industry, get it to the people who can benefit from having it the most, and file it so it is easy to find when needed. Executive secretaries handle these tasks with ease.

It is difficult to replace an accomplished executive secretary, but some of them do their jobs so well that they eventually end up in the management ranks. As they make valuable contributions to their companies or organizations, these executive secretaries use their jobs as a springboard to move up to a management position as the company or organization expands. That helps open up more executive secretary positions for other ambitious people.

At one time, around the turn of the 21st century, leaders in business and industry thought that money could be saved by not hiring executive secretaries, or least not hiring as many as in the past. That thinking was shown to be very shortsighted. With less high-level secretarial help, key administrative tasks fell to executives themselves, who were slow to get these jobs done, if they completed them at all. As a result, these executives were far less productive. Forcing executives to do the work once handled by an executive secretary cut into the time of those in upper management to do strategic planning, oversee departments under their purview, and pursue new ventures that might yield substantial benefits for the organization. The company's bottom line suffered.

More than 400,000 new businesses are started in the United States every year. Not all those new businesses need executive secretaries at first, but many of them do. Start-ups are a fertile ground for people looking to land jobs as executive secretaries, and it gives you a chance to get into a business on the ground floor.

GETTING STARTED

RARELY DOES A PERSON STEP RIGHT OUT of school and into a job as an executive secretary. Most people who are hired as executive secretaries have substantial experience, and a track record backed up with solid recommendations. You get that experience by working first as a secretary, and there is a big difference between being a secretary and being an executive secretary.

Secretaries file, type, answer phones, and make appointments. They may do this for one person in the office or an entire department. As time goes on, a secretary's role may grow, but that job will never carry the same responsibilities as that of an executive secretary. Executive secretaries handle complex tasks, making decisions and judgment calls, and resolving issues as they arise.

For a person who aspires to be an executive secretary, the best place to land a position as a secretary is in an office that has an adept executive secretary on staff. That person will show you how the job is done. This will allow you to get the experience you need as a secretary and see firsthand how an executive secretary operates.

At some companies, where the work is substantial, executive secretaries have assistants. As an assistant to an executive secretary, you can get some hands-on training for the job as executive secretary. You have to spend about a year or so as a secretary, and do exceptional work in that position, to be considered for a promotion to assistant to the executive secretary. If you are given this promotion, you are being groomed to become an executive secretary one day, and this will be an important part of your résumé.

Once you learn all you can, you will probably have to move to another company to land the executive secretary job you want. That is because most executive secretaries are entrenched in their jobs and are not replaced until they retire.

At the start of your career, you need to decide on the field you would like to concentrate in. Whether it is in the corporate sphere – at a bank, a pharmaceutical company, an insurance company – in education at a college or local school district, or at a religious organization, a government agency, or a nonprofit, you have a better chance of moving up from a secretarial position to executive secretary if you stay in the same field. Those hiring executive secretaries value a candidate's administrative experience as much as they do that candidate's knowledge of the industry. For a CEO, director, or president of an organization, it is simply easier not to have to teach an executive secretary the ins and outs of a particular industry.

Not all jobs for executive secretaries are advertised – this is where networking comes in. By joining organizations like the International Association of Administrative Professionals (IAAP), you can get to know other people who work as executive secretaries. They can tell you as soon as jobs become available and who to talk with about the job. The IAAP has more than 20 local area networks (chapters) throughout the United States and Canada. One of the organization's primary goals, besides education, is networking.

ASSOCIATIONS

■ **International Association of Administrative Professionals (IAAP)**
https://www.iaap-hq.org

■ **C-Suite Executive Support Professionals**
http://www.c-sesp.org

■ **American Society of Administrative Professionals (ASAP)**
http://www.asaporg.com

■ **The Association of Executive and Administrative Professionals (AEAP)**
http://www.theaeap.com

■ **Association of Legal Administrators (ALA)**
http://www.alanet.org

■ **Association for Healthcare Administrative Professionals (AHCAP)**
http://www.ahcap.org

■ **National Healthcareer Association (NHA)**
http://www.nhanow.com

■ **American Association of Medical Assistants (AAMA)**
http://www.aama-ntl.org

■ **NALS: The Association for Legal Professionals**
http://www.nals.org

■ **Legal Secretaries International**
http://www.legalsecretaries.org

PERIODICALS

■ **Executive Secretary Magazine**

■ **OfficePro**

■ **AdminAdvantage**

■ **Corporate Secretary**

■ **Assistant Edge**

■ **Legal Secretary Journal**

■ **The Legal Secretary**

■ **Executive PA**

WEBSITES

■ **OfficeNinjas**
https://officeninjas.com

■ **All Things Admin**
http://allthingsadmin.com

■ **The Effective Admin**
http://www.theeffectiveadmin.com

■ **Global PA Association**
http://www.globalpa-association.com

■ **Personal-Assistant-Tips.com**
http://www.personal-assistant-tips.com

■ **Office Dynamics International**
https://officedynamics.com/blog

■ **Administrative Professional Today**
http://www.adminprotoday.com

SCHOOLS

■ **Alamance Community College**
**https://www.alamancecc.edu/arts
-and-sciences-site/office-administration**

■ **Kansas City Kansas Community College (KCKCC)**
**http://www.kckcc.edu/programs/degrees-certificates
/technical-certificates/administrative-office
-professional**

■ **International Association of Administrative
Professionals (IAAP)**
http://www.iaap-hq.org

www.ingramcontent.com/pod-product-compliance
Lightning Source LLC
Chambersburg PA
CBHW061235180526
45170CB00003B/1314